# THE MERRY CHRISTMAS BOOK

Compiled by Jill Bennett with help from Archie Millar

Illustrated by Peter Lawson

HIPPO

Hippo Books
Scholastic Publications Limited
London

## For Suzanne, Kate and Ian

We recommend only the use of the following glues: UHU Stick, Pritt Stick, Scotch Pen, paste and children's glue, Stephen's Trufix paste, Copydex Childsplay, Gloy children's glue.

Scholastic Publications Ltd.,
10 Earlham Street, London WC2H 9RX, UK

Scholastic Inc.,
730 Broadway, New York, NY 10003, USA

Scholastic TAB Publications Ltd.,
123 Newkirk Road, Richmond Hill, Ontario L4C 3G5, Canada

Ashton Scholastic Pty. Ltd.,
PO Box 579, Gosford, New South Wales, Australia

Ashton Scholastic Ltd.,
165 Marua Road, Panmure, Auckland 6, New Zealand

First published by Scholastic Publications Limited, 1987

This collection copyright © Scholastic Publications Limited, 1987
Illustrations copyright © Peter Lawson

The publishers and compiler would like to thank the following for their kind permission to include the following copyright material in this book: *Ten Little Christmas Trees* by Rodney Bennett, copyright © Rodney Bennett, and reproduced from *Seeing and Doing Book II* published by Thames Methuen; *Lullaby Carol* by Gerard Benson, copyright © Gerard Benson, and reproduced by his kind permission from *Child Education* published by Scholastic Publications Ltd.; *Big Fat Rosie's Christmas Present* by Mary Danby Calvert, copyright © Mary Calvert, 1972, and reproduced by her kind permission from *Big Fat Rosie* published by Knight Books; *High in Heaven* and *Mary's Song* both by Charles Causley, copyright © Charles Causley, and reproduced by kind permission of the publishers from *The Gift of a Lamb* published by Robson Books Ltd.; *Parcel* by Jean Chapman, copyright © Jean Chapman, and reproduced by kind permission of the publishers from *The Sugar-Plum Christmas Book* published by Hodder and Stoughton (Australia) Pty. Ltd.; *Christmas Eve* by Arnold Lobel, copyright © by Arnold Lobel, and reproduced by kind permission of the publishers from *Frog and Toad All Year* published by William Heinemann Ltd. UK and Harper and Row Publishers, USA; *It's Christmas* by Wes Magee, copyright © Wes Magee, and reproduced by his kind permission from *A Shooting Star* published by Basil Blackwell Ltd.; *Christmas Dinner* by Michael Rosen, copyright © Michael Rosen and reproduced by kind permission of the publishers from *Quick Let's Get Out Of Here* published by André Deutsch Ltd.

*Every effort has been made to trace the copyright owners of the material set in this book. If, despite this, we have inadvertently failed to identify any borrowed work, we would be grateful if this could be brought to our attention for correction at the first opportunity.*

ISBN 0 590 70726 4

Made and printed by Mateu Cromo, Madrid, Spain
Typeset in Times by AKM Associates (UK) Ltd., Southall, London UB2 5NG

# CONTENTS

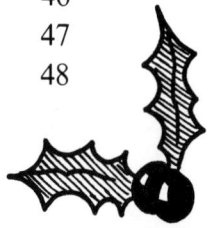

# Count Down to Christmas

It's nearly Christmas so why not make an Advent calendar to help you count down to the big day? Advent calendars are a traditional Christmas custom. In most of them, a door is opened each day of Advent to reveal a Christmas picture. This one is slightly different and is very popular in Sweden. Perhaps you could make it for your parents or for a friend or brother or sister. When they open each drawer they will have a lovely surprise!

**REMEMBER! Matches are VERY dangerous! You must NEVER play with them!**

### You will need:

★ 24 empty matchboxes (ask grown-ups to help you collect them)
★ glue
★ thin white card or white paint
★ scissors
★ coloured self-adhesive stickers *or* sticky paper *or* felt-tip pens
★ ribbon *or* cotton thread *or* beads

### What you do:

1 Lay your matchboxes in a long row with their sides touching.
2 Carefully glue them together and then leave them on one side to dry.
3 To strengthen the strip, glue thin strips of card to the boxes so that they overlap the joins. Now leave it to dry!
4 Paint each box white, or alternatively, cover them with thin white card.

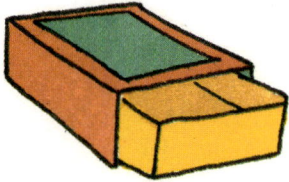

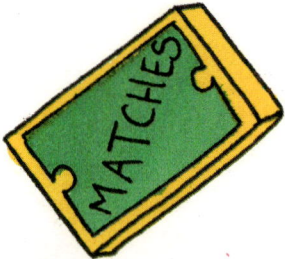

5 When the paint or glue is dry, decorate the boxes with Christmas designs. You can use self-adhesive stickers or you may prefer to draw your own designs on each box with felt-tip pens.

6 Using a felt-tip pen, number the boxes from 1 to 24, writing the number on the drawers and starting from the top.

7 Take out each of the trays and glue a bead or a loop of thread to one end. This acts as the handle of the drawer.

8 Now, inside each tray, put a surprise! This could be a special message or Christmas picture you have made; a picture you have cut from an old Christmas card; a tiny thimble; a dried flower or even a sweet! Try to think of twenty-four different surprises to make your Advent calendar really special.

9 Now carefully put all the trays back into the boxes.

10 Put a loop of ribbon on the top box so that the whole strip can be hung up. Make sure this is glued very securely or your calendar will fall down!

*Now you have a wonderful Advent calendar, and starting from 1 December, you can open a drawer each day until Christmas!*

# Advent Candle

*On the last four Sundays before Christmas many people think about the "Advent", or coming of Jesus, and in churches and some homes, candles are lit.*

*On December 1, light your candle and let it burn down to the mark for the next day. Then you can light your candle each night in the same way until Christmas Eve when you can keep it alight until it burns right down.*

**You will need**:

★ a tall white candle
★ a ruler
★ red nail varnish
★ a knife (don t use one that is too sharp!)

**What you do**:

1 Using your ruler  divide the candle into twenty-four equal parts, starting at least 5cm from the bottom.
2 Gently mark each of the points on the candle with the knife.
3 Very carefully draw a line arour the candle on each mark with the nail varnish.
4 Starting from the top, write the number 1 by the first line and so on down to 24, as shown on the illustration.
5 Place your candle in a candlestick and now you have an Advent Candle of your own!

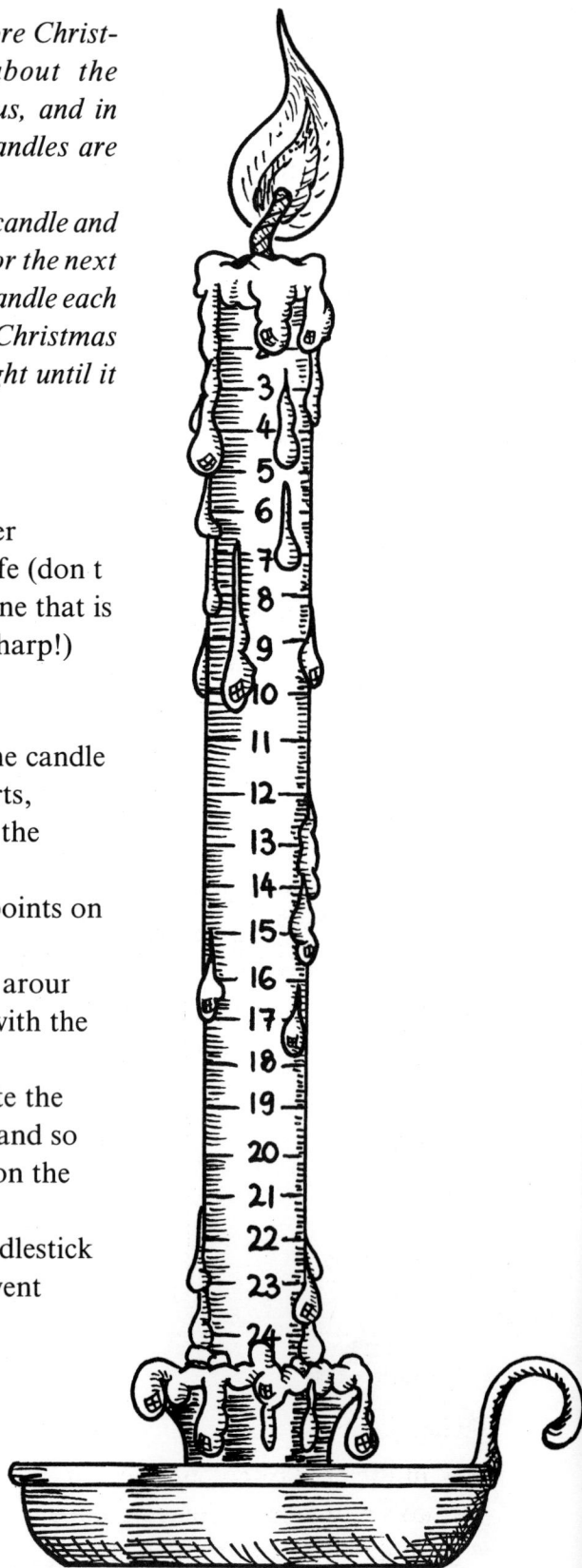

# HERBAL BATH SACHETS

*Bath sachets are small bags filled with dried, scented herbs such as lavender, rosemary or lemon thyme. If a bag is tied to the bath tap so that the hot water runs over it while filling the bath, it will scent the water.*

**You will need:**

★ dried herbs (if you don't grow your own you can buy them from a health food store or herb shop)
★ thin material such as cheese cloth or muslin
★ strong cotton thread
★ coloured tape, ribbon or bias binding

**What you do:**

1 Cut out pieces of the material about 12cm square.
2 Put some dried herbs into the centre of each square.
3 Gather each into a bag and tie it at the top with the thread.
4 Make a loop out of tape or ribbon on each one so that it can hang over the tap.

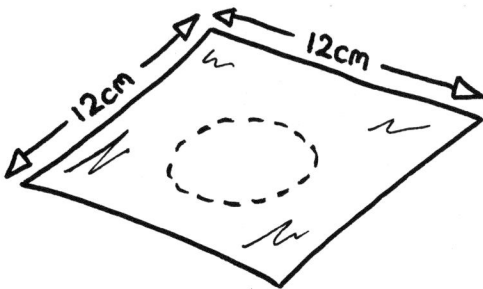

## Tags Too!

MERRY Christmas · Happy Christmas · To K.L. from M.

*Personalize your presents by designing your own gift tags. These are good things to make and sell for charity too!*

**You will need:**

★ thin card or stiff coloured paper
★ scissors or pinking shears
★ self-adhesive shapes and labels or sticky paper
★ coloured thread or ribbon
★ hole punch

**What you do:**

1 Cut the card or coloured paper into small pieces. You can make any shape you want such as crackers, trees or even Christmas puddings. If you cut out your shape with pinking shears it will make a zig-zag edge.
2 Decorate each one with adhesive shapes and labels.
3 Punch a hole and loop through some ribbon or thread.
4 Write on your greeting and attach the label to your present!

Happy Christmas Noddy

7

# Make your own Christmas
# TREASURE CHEST

*Everybody loves giving presents at Christmas and now you can make yours extra special by making a pretty box to put your gifts in! The best way to make a box is out of one piece of card or paper which is folded into shape. You can use the diagram opposite as your pattern.*

*Each square has a side of 6cm. You could* either *trace this one directly and then transfer it onto card or coloured paper.* Or, *if you have some squared paper (like your maths book at school), you could use the pattern as a guide and draw out one with larger sided squares.*

**You will need:**

★ card, coloured paper, squared paper
★ colouring pencils and felt-tip pens
★ scissors
★ a ruler
★ glue

**What you do:**

1 Cut along the outside lines carefully.
2 Fold along each dotted line to make a sharp edge. All folds should be inwards. (You might find it easier to place a ruler on the dotted line and fold against the ruler.)
3 If you want to decorate your box, it is easier to do so before you glue it together. You could draw holly, Santas, snow men, stars and all sorts of festive things.
4 Carefully glue the tabs INSIDE the box. Then wait for it to dry before you put your gift inside!

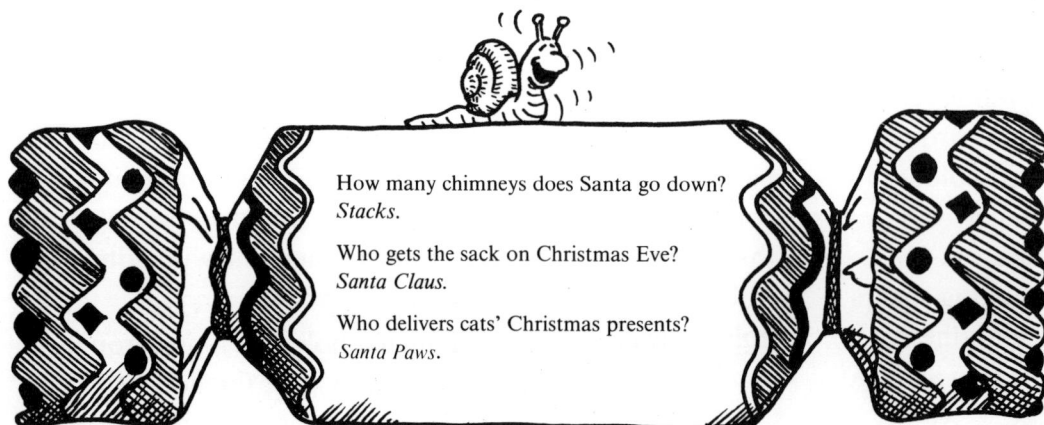

How many chimneys does Santa go down?
*Stacks.*

Who gets the sack on Christmas Eve?
*Santa Claus.*

Who delivers cats' Christmas presents?
*Santa Paws.*

6cm

6cm

# Cheerful Christmas Cards to Make

*Cards are a way of telling people far away that you are thinking of them at Christmas time.*

**You will need:**

- ★ thin card
- ★ felt-tip pens and colours
- ★ scissors
- ★ coloured paper
- ★ blunt knife
- ★ ruler

**What you do:**

1 Cut your card to the size you want.
2 Fold the card in half and press a crease along the centre with your ruler edge.
3 Make your design on the front of the card. Here are some ideas:

You can cut this shape from coloured paper and stick it onto your card. Use coloured stickers to make the decorations if you don't want to colour them in. When put together you have a Christmas tree like this:

ANOTHER DESIGN TO MAKE WOULD BE TO DRAW ROUND YOUR TREE SHAPE ON THE BLANK CARD. CUT OUT THE SHAPE AS SHOWN. YOU MIGHT NEED A GROWN UPS HELP WITH THIS!
NOW YOU HAVE A WINDOW IN YOUR CARD!
WITH THE CARD FOLDED, COLOUR THE AREA BETWEEN YOUR TREE STENCIL OR PATTERN IT. DECORATE THE FRONT OF YOUR CARD. NOW ADD YOUR GREETING TO THE FRONT AND INSIDE OF YOUR CARD.

10

# How to make an Envelope

*Now you've made your cards you will need to have some envelopes to put them in!*

**You will need:**

★ a sheet of paper slightly wider than your card and

about twice as long
★ scissors
★ glue

**What you do:**

1 Draw around the shape of your card first and then add the flaps. The diagram below should help you:

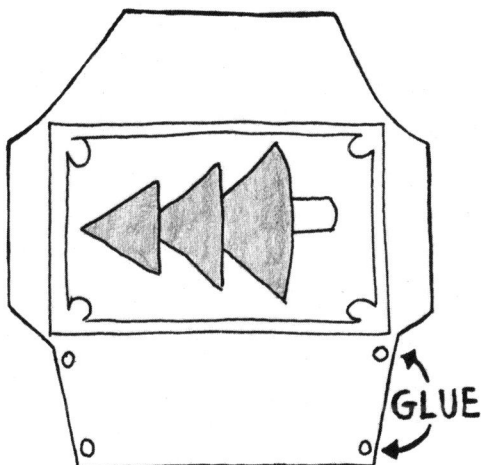

The dotted line represents the size of your card.

2 Now you have to fold your card. First fold the sides in. Then fold the bottom up. Now fold the top down.
3 Put tiny blobs of glue in the places indicated by circles on the diagram and press down.
4 When the glue is dry, you can pop your card inside the envelope!

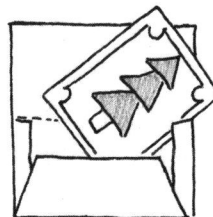

GLUE

# POMPOMS

*Pompoms are a great way of making parcels look extra exciting!*

**You will need:**

★ metallic paper in about 6 different colours
★ glue
★ scissors

**What you do:**

1 Cut the paper into shapes (such as stars or flowers) of 6 different sizes.

2 Put a thin line of glue right down the middle of each shape and press them together as shown. You can either use all the same colour or any combination you want.
3 When the glue has dried, carefully bend the edges upwards.
4 Now your pompom is ready to be stuck onto your parcel! It is best to use a small piece of double−sided sticky tape but you can bend round a strip of ordinary tape if you haven't any.

# Fun with Words at Christmas

## CHRISTMAS SONGS SLIP-UP

One of Santa's helpers was on his way to a concert carrying the words of some well-known carols and songs. Suddenly he slipped on the ice and they went EVERYWHERE! He managed to get the titles or first lines together but couldn't unscramble the letters or put the words of each one in the right order.

**How quickly can you help him sort them out?**

1. het nsig krHa lehard slagen
2. ycti ni ecOn diavD's alyor
3. gthin yhol tihgn nleSit
4. ertih ghnit yb rdesphesh eWilh tcdehaw cfsolk
5. sedon eth pluhodR edr enidrere
6. ni a granme wyAa
7. yoknde itLetl
8. no Go natimuon ti ltel het
9. lraoc obowcy ehT
10. byo dah a aMry riVing heT byba
11. rtsif fo hiCrtamss yda nO hte
12. rermy oyu shwi a smCirhtas eW

**How many words can you make from the word CHRISTMAS?**

Here are a few we found to start you off:
Stars, cats, hiss, mass, hats.

**Here is an example of a kind of CHRISTMAS CROSSTICK using the word ANGEL:**

santA
traiN
sinG
spongE
labeL

Try making some more words out of the word ANGEL.
Can you do the same with PRESENT and YULE LOG?

Look closely at these two pictures. There are ten differences. Can you spot them all?

Look carefully at the four baubles. Three are identical. But can you spot which one is the odd one out?

A          B          C          D

# Santa in the Chimney

**A jump-up Santa for you to make!**

## You will need:

- ★ a stick or dowel rod about 40cm long
- ★ a clean yogurt pot or small cream tub
- ★ old tights or a knee-high stocking
- ★ scraps of red and black material
- ★ buttons or other material scraps for Santa's features
- ★ cotton wool or similar material for stuffing
- ★ paper
- ★ cotton thread or wool
- ★ glue
- ★ scissors

## What you do:

1 Cut one leg from the tights *or* you can use one knee-high stocking.

2 Cut the leg part to about 30cm long and tie one end with the cotton. (You won't have to do this if you are using a knee-high stocking.)

3 Turn the leg inside out.

4 Make a ball out of cotton wool and push it into the tied end. This makes Santa's head.

5 Poke one end of the stick into the cotton wool and tie round the neck with wool or cotton thread. Make sure this is tight. (fig. 1.)

6 With the point of your scissors, *very carefully* make a small round hole in the bottom of the plastic pot. *Mind your fingers!*

7 Now push the other end of the stick through the hole. (fig. 2.)

8 Going back to the tights, pull out arm shapes on either side about a centimetre from Santa's neck. Poke in a little cotton wool and tie, just as you did the head. (fig.3.)

9 Glue the open end of the tight leg round the top outside edge of the pot. (fig. 4.)

10 Cut out small fabric pieces in the shape of two eyes and a nose (or you can use buttons). Glue these into place. Then cut a mouth shape and glue this too. (fig. 5.)

11 Make a beard from the cotton wool and glue this just below Santa's mouth.

12 While Santa's face is drying, make a coat from the red material. Cut a semi-circle and then wrap this carefully around the body and glue round the neck and down the front. Add a black belt. (fig. 6.)

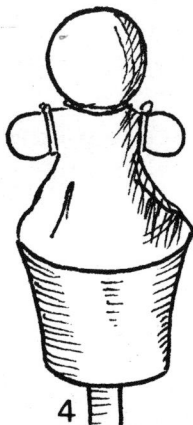

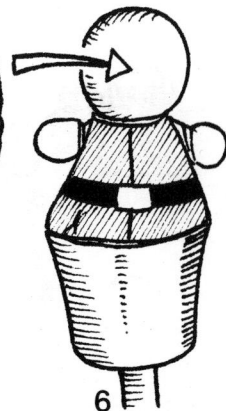

13 Cut a strip of paper to fit around the yogurt pot and colour this with pens or crayons so that it looks like a chimney. Then carefully glue it around the pot.

14 Decorate the chimney with snow by gluing cotton wool around the top edge of the pot over the join with the tights. (fig. 7.)

*Santa in the chimney works a bit like a jack-in-the-box. Push the stick up and down to make him pop out of, and back down into, the chimney.*

# Christmas Eve

**by Arnold Lobel**

On Christmas Eve Toad cooked a big dinner. He decorated the tree.

"Frog is late," said Toad.

"I am worried," said Toad. "What if something terrible has happened?" said Toad. "What if Frog has fallen into a deep hole and cannot get out? I will never see him again!"

Toad looked at his clock. He remembered it was broken. The hands of the clock did not move. Toad opened the front door. He looked out into the night. Frog was not there.

"What if Frog is being
chased by a big animal with many
sharp teeth? What if he is being eaten
up?" cried Toad. "My friend and I will
never have another Christmas
together!"

Toad opened the door once more.
Frog was not on the path.

Toad found some rope in the cellar.
"I will pull Frog out of the hole with
this," said Toad.

"What if Frog is lost in the woods?"
said Toad. "What if he is cold and wet
and hungry?"

Toad found a lantern in the attic. "Frog will see this light. I will show him the way out of the woods," said Toad.

Toad found a frying pan in the kitchen. "I will hit the big animal with this," said Toad. "All of his teeth will fall out. Frog, do not worry," cried Toad. "I am coming to help you!"

Toad ran out of his house. There was Frog.

"Hello, Toad," he said. "I am very sorry to be late. I was wrapping your present."

"You are not at the bottom of a hole?" asked Toad.

"No," said Frog.

"You are not lost in the woods?" asked Toad.

"No," said Frog.

"You are not being eaten by a big animal?" asked Toad.

"No," said Frog. "Not at all."

"Oh, Frog," said Toad, "I am so glad to be spending Christmas with you."

Toad opened his present from Frog. It was a beautiful new clock. The two friends sat by the fire. The hands of the clock moved to show the hours of a merry Christmas Eve.

# CALYPSO CAROL

Long time ago in Bethlehem,
So the Holy Bible say,
Mary's boy-child Jesus Christ,
He born on Chrisamus Day!

*Mary had a boy-child, Jesus Christ,*
*He's a born on Chrisamus Day,*
*my my, my my!*
*Mary had a boy-child, Jesus Christ,*
*He's a born on Chrisamus Day!*

While shepherds watched their flocks by night,
They see a bright new shining star,
Then the herald choir sing,
The music seem to come from afar.

*Mary had a boy-child, Jesus Christ . . .*

Now Joseph and his wife Mary,
Came to Bethlehem that night,
They find no place for to born she child;
Not a single room was in sight.

*Mary had a boy-child, Jesus Christ . . .*

By-n-by they find a little nook,
In a stable all forlorn,
And in a manger cold and dark,
Mary's little boy-child was born.

*Mary had a boy-child, Jesus Christ . . .*

(repeat chorus and first verse)

**Traditional West Indian carol**

# Yuletide Rhymes

## On Christmas Day

There was a pig
Went out to dig,
Christmas Day, Christmas Day,
There was a pig
Went out to dig
On Christmas Day in the morning.
There was a sow
Went out to plough,
On Christmas Day, Christmas Day,
There was a sow
Went out to plough
On Christmas Day in the morning.
There was a sparrow
Went out to harrow,
Christmas Day, Christmas Day,
There was a sparrow
Went out to harrow
On Christmas Day in the morning.

There was a drake
Went out to rake,
Christmas Day, Christmas Day,
There was a drake
Went out to rake
On Christmas Day in the morning.
There was a crow
Went out to sow,
Christmas Day, Christmas Day,
There was a crow
Went out to sow
On Christmas Day in the morning.
There was a sheep
Went out to reap,
Christmas Day, Christmas Day,
There was a sheep
Went out to reap
On Christmas Day in the morning.

**anon.**

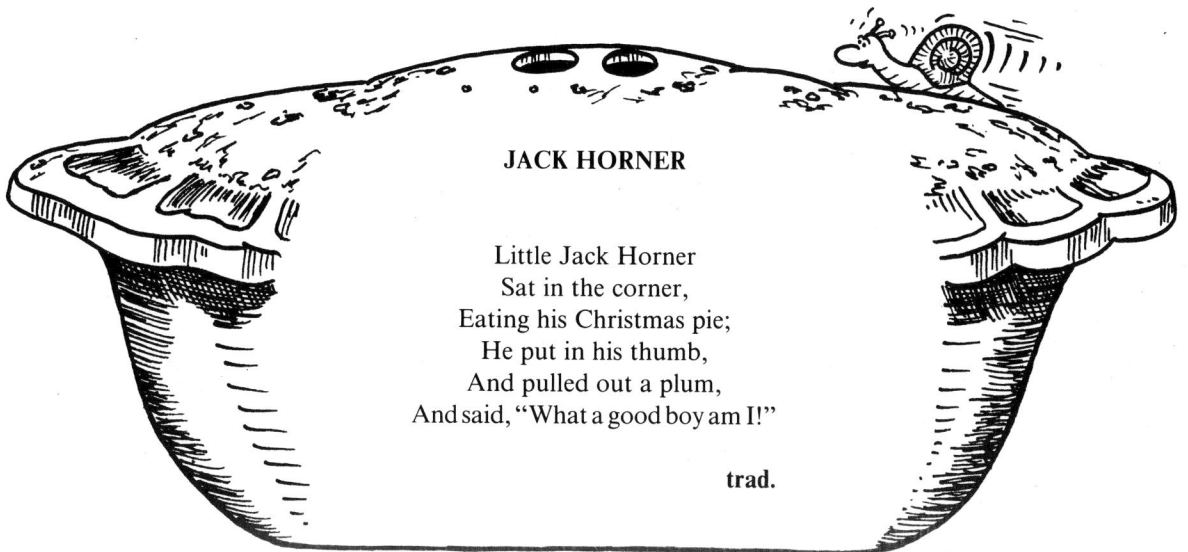

### JACK HORNER

Little Jack Horner
Sat in the corner,
Eating his Christmas pie;
He put in his thumb,
And pulled out a plum,
And said, "What a good boy am I!"

**trad.**

# Nativity Finger Puppets

*Puppet shows are always fun. Why not entertain your Christmas visitors with a Nativity play?*

**You will need:**

- ★ scraps of felt in assorted colours including flesh colour
- ★ felt-tip pens
- ★ fabric glue
- ★ scissors
- ★ scraps of wool
- ★ oddments of braid and lace, beads and sequins for decoration

**What you do:**

1 Using picture 1 as a guide, cut out 2 basic shapes for each figure. You will need Mary, Joseph, the Three Kings and shepherds.

2 Cut out faces from the flesh coloured felt.

3 Draw on the facial features with felt-tip pens.

4 Glue on the faces — see picture 2.

5 With the *wrong* sides together, sew the back of each figure to the front using small stitches. If you prefer, you can stick the front and back together with fabric glue.

6 Turn the puppets right side out and stick on scraps of wool or dark felt for the hair, as in picture 3.

7 Use lace scraps to make head-dresses.

8 Decorate the puppets with the sequins, braid or beads to create different characters.

9 Using picture 4 as a guide, cut out the shape of the baby Jesus from the white felt.

10 When you have stuck on the baby's face, place it in front of Mary as in picture 5, *or* you could make a tiny cradle from a matchbox and put the baby in this. In this case, you can cover Him with some white scraps of material.

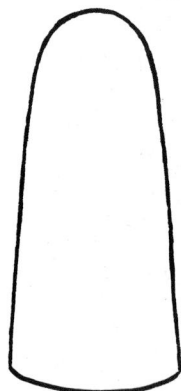

1

2

3

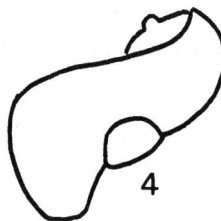

4

5

# Lullaby Carol

Mary sang to her pretty baby
*Sleep, little one, sleep,*
And all the bright angels
Of heaven sang with her
*Sleep, little one, sleep.*

Some shepherds heard them in the fields
Where they were watching their sheep,
They went to the stable
And joined in the carol
*Sleep, little one, sleep.*

From faraway lands came kings
Over the mountains so steep,
With gifts for the baby
They joined in the carol
*Sleep, little one, sleep.*

*Sleep, little one, sleep,*
Close your eyes and don't peep,
Your father and mother
Are watching your cradle
*Sleep, little one, sleep.*

**Gerard Benson**

# CHRISTMAS WHIZ

**SLIP ON ICE GO BACK 5** — 62.

**SANTA UNWELL — MISS A TURN** — 59.

64. 63. 62. 61. 60. 59. 58.

**SANTA STOPPED FOR SPEEDING — MISS TWO MOVES** — 57.

**REINDEER FEELING FRISKY GO FORWARD 4** — 55.

**FOOD LEFT FOR REINDEER GO FORWARD 3** — 47.

**CAROL SINGING VERY GOOD — MOVE TO SQUARE 54** — 51.

47. 48. 49. 50. 51. 52. 53. 54.

**CLEAR SKY, GO QUICKLY TO Nº 30** — 26.

**REINDEER UNWELL — MISS TWO MOVES** — 21.

26. 25. 24. 23. 22. 21. 20. 19.

18.

**SANTA HITS CHIMNEY — GO BACK 3** — 17.

16.

**NO SPEED LIMIT — GO FORWARD 4** — 10.

**ADDRESSES EASY TO READ — GO FORWARD 2** — 14.

8. 9. 10. 11. 12. 13. 14. 15.

# High in the Heaven

High in the Heaven
A gold star burns
Lighting our way
As the great world turns.

Silver the frost
It shines on the stem
As we now journey
To Bethlehem.

White is the ice
At our feet as we tread,
Pointing a path
To the manger-bed.

**Charles Causley**

# Colouring Tree

**DECORATE THIS TREE BY COLOURING IN THE SHAPES**

# MARY'S SONG

Sleep, King Jesus,
Your royal bed
Is made of hay
In a cattle-shed.
Sleep, King Jesus,
Do not fear,
Joseph is watching
And waiting near.

Warm in the wintry air
You lie,
The ox and the donkey
Standing by,
With summer eyes
They seem to say:
Welcome, Jesus,
On Christmas Day!

Sleep, King Jesus:
Your diamond crown
High in the sky
Where stars look down.
Let your reign
Of love begin,
That all the world
May enter in.

**Charles Causley**

# CRACKING Christmas Codes

Santa has been asked in code for some presents. Can you work out what the presents are?

To crack the code, Santa has worked out that

1 = A, 2 = B, 3 = C, 4 = D and so on.

You will need to write down the letters of the alphabet and the numbers 1 to 26 next to them. Use this code breaker to help Santa solve the problem below:

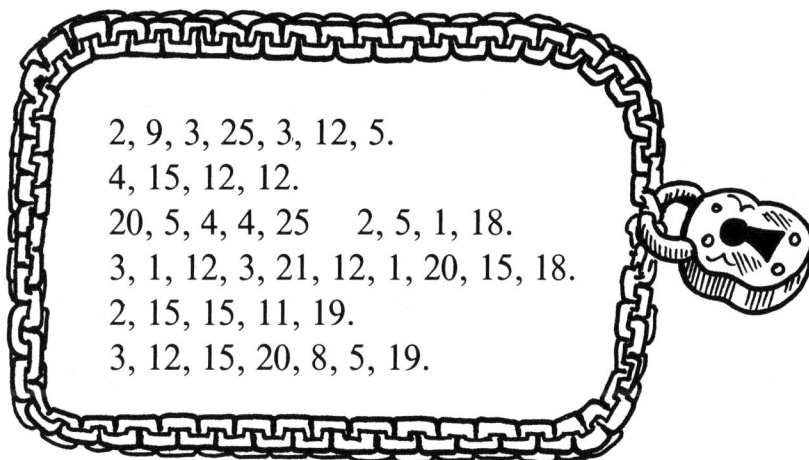

2, 9, 3, 25, 3, 12, 5.
4, 15, 12, 12.
20, 5, 4, 4, 25    2, 5, 1, 18.
3, 1, 12, 3, 21, 12, 1, 20, 15, 18.
2, 15, 15, 11, 19.
3, 12, 15, 20, 8, 5, 19.

**Can you work out the Christmas words?**
Take the first letter of each picture and write it in the box below:

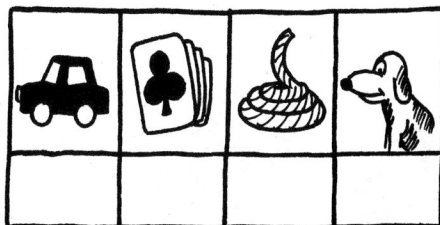

# Christmas Cooking

It is always fun to cook – especially at Christmas! Before you start:

**REMEMBER**:

WASH YOUR HANDS BEFORE YOU START!
WEAR AN APRON!
ASK AN ADULT TO LIGHT THE OVEN!
USE OVEN GLOVES TO HOLD ANYTHING HOT!
DO THE WASHING UP WHEN YOU'VE FINISHED!

## LEMON BISCUITS

*You could hang these on your Christmas tree and eat them for Christmas tea or you could wrap them in foil, put them in your Christmas Treasure Chest and give them as a present!*

**You will need:**

225g PLAIN FLOUR
A LEMON
100g CASTOR SUGAR
ONE SMALL EGG
100g MARGARINE

BOWL AND WOODEN SPOON
FLOUR SIFTER
FORK OR WHISK
GRATER
BISCUIT CUTTERS OR CUP
BAKING TRAY
ROLLING PIN
PASTRY BOARD
OVEN GLOVES

**What you do:**

1 *Ask an adult* to pre-heat the oven to 190C (375F) *or* Gas Mark 5.
2 Beat the margarine and sugar together with a wooden spoon until it is pale and fluffy.

3 In a cup, beat the egg and then add it to the mixture.

4 Sift the flour into the mixture.

5 Grate the peel from the lemon and add to the mixture.

6 Mix everything well together. Now you have your biscuit dough.

7 With your hands, make the dough into a ball.

8 Place the dough in the fridge for about 15 minutes.

9 Now roll out the dough on a floured board so that it is about half a centimetre thick.

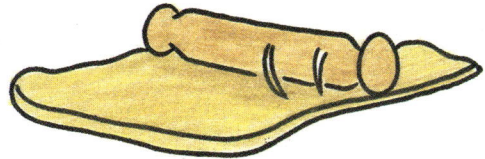

10 Using biscuit cutters or a knife, cut the dough into shapes such as stars, snowmen, pieces of holly, etc. (You can also use the rim of a cup to make round biscuits.)

11 Put the biscuits on a flat, greased baking tray.

12 *Ask an adult* to place the tray in the centre of the oven to bake for about 10 minutes. *Check to see that the biscuits are going brownish but that the edges aren't burning!*

13 Turn off the oven and *ask an adult to remove the baking tray from the oven!*

14 Leave the biscuits on one side to cool.

# SUGAR MICE

*These look very pretty but NEVER make these on your own! ALWAYS have an adult with you!*

## You will need:

ingredients: 450g granulated sugar
150ml water
pinch of cream of tartar
food colouring (such as cochineal)
silver balls
string

utensils: baking sheet, spatula, saucepan, wooden spoon, sugar thermometer

## What you do:

1 Pour the water into a saucepan and *ask an adult* to place it over a gentle heat. Pour in the sugar and stir all the time with a wooden spoon until the sugar is dissolved.

2 Add a pinch of cream of tartar and *ask an adult* carefully to place the thermometer in the saucepan.

3 Bring the mixture to the boil. Keep boiling until the thermometer reads 116C (240F) which should take about 2 or 3 minutes. (If you haven't got a thermometer, you can always test the mixture by dropping a little of it into a cup of cold water: it should form a soft ball.)

4 *Ask an adult* to remove the pan from the heat.

5 Carefully pour the mixture onto a cold baking sheet and leave for a minute or so to cool off.

6 Using the spatula, scrape in the sides of the mixture and slap it around with your hands until it begins to look white.

7 If you want to make pink mice as well, divide the mixture in half and colour one batch with one or two drops of colouring. *Watch out!* The colour is *very* strong!

8 Knead the mixture with your hands and mould it into mouse shapes.

9 Add silver balls for the eyes and string for the tails.

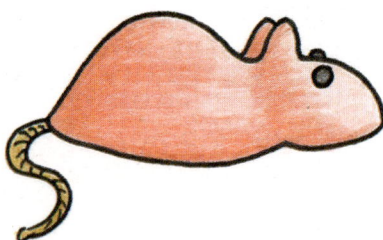

## TURKISH DELIGHT

*You could wrap this in wax paper and put it into your Christmas Treasure Chest! It will also keep well in an airtight tin.*

**You will need:**

ingredients:  450g granulated sugar
25g gelatine
300ml water
cornflour
icing sugar
lemon juice *or* rosewater
utensils:  shallow tin, 2 saucepans, knife,
wooden spoon, wooden board, clean cloth

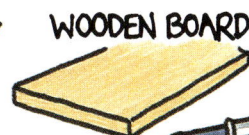

**What you do:**

1 Pour half the water into one of the saucepans.
2 *Ask an adult* to place the saucepan over a low heat and pour in the gelatine, mixing until it is completely dissolved.
3 Pour the rest of the water into the other saucepan and *ask an adult* to place this pan over heat. Pour in the sugar and stir it constantly with a wooden spoon.
4 *Ask an adult* to stand with you whilst the sugar water comes to the boil.
5 *Ask an adult* to remove the sugar water from the heat and add the gelatine.
6 Simmer the mixture over a low heat for 15-20 minutes, stirring all the time.
7 *Ask an adult* to remove the pan from the heat and stir in either lemon juice or rose water to add flavouring.
8 Cover the saucepan and leave it on one side to cool for about 15 minutes.
9 Using a spoon, skim off any skin that may have formed on top.
10 Rinse out the tin with cold water and pour in the mixture.
11 Leave this to set and then rub cornflour into the surface.
12 Dip a knife into the icing sugar and cut the Turkish Delight into cubes.
13 Rub in some cornflour over each piece and then toss the cubes in icing sugar in the clean cloth.

# Big Fat Rosie's Christmas Present

**by Mary Danby Calvert**

There were only a few days to go before Christmas, and Big Fat Rosie still hadn't bought a present for Turnip Tom. She had bought a pair of woolly gloves for old Harry, and a jingly bell for Alexander the pig to ring when he was hungry. For Lollipop, the big carthorse, there was a green plastic water bucket, and for Annabel the pony, a big bag of carrots. She had knitted some yellow ear-warmers for Maisie the cow. But she couldn't think *what* to get for Turnip Tom.

Big Fat Rosie sat down in the kitchen on her rocking chair and thought and thought. The rocking chair creaked, like this

and soon Rosie, tired out by all her thinking, fell fast asleep. Before long, she was snoring, like this

and as she slept and snored, she had a dream . . .

In her dream, a large bakery van drew up outside the farmhouse. On the side there was a notice. It said: *Happy Christmas, Big Fat Rosie.* She ran out to the road and opened the door of the van. She could hardly believe her eyes. Inside the van were trays and trays of delicious-looking cream buns. Big Fat Rosie giggled, like this

for, of course, cream buns were her favourite food. But, just as she was about to taste one of the buns, the kitchen clock struck three, like this

and Big Fat Rosie woke up with a start. She was back in her rocking chair — and the cream buns had vanished. At the thought of missing such a feast, Big Fat Rosie began to cry, like this

OWO = WO = WOO
OWO = WOO!

and all her chins wobbled with misery.

Now Big Fat Rosie cried such huge great sopping wet tears that in a few minutes the kitchen was deep in water, and all the rugs were floating about. The door mat drifted slowly past her and sank to the floor under the kitchen table. Then something went bump-bump against Big Fat Rosie's ankles, and she looked down. Turnip Tom's old slippers! She stopped crying and picked them up. They were soaking wet, and all the colours had run into each other. Whatever would Turnip Tom say?

Turnip Tom had heard all the crying and came in to see what the matter was. He looked at his slippers and sighed, like this

WHEE - YEW

Then he put them on. The water had made them shrink — they were much too small for him now — and he hobbled around the kitchen in them,

looking as if he were doing a funny sort of dance.

Big Fat Rosie said she was very, very sorry, but there was a secret sort of smile on her face as she hurried to put on her great big coat and her winter boots. Big Fat Rosie was going Christmas shopping.

As she left the farmhouse and walked down to the shoe shop in the village, she hummed a happy little tune, like this

DUM = DUM = DI = DUM
DUMMETTY = DUMMETTY
DUM = DI
DUM

At the shop, she bought a beautiful pair of red, suede, fleecy-lined slippers. This Christmas, Turnip Tom would have the warmest toes in the whole world.

And so he did. When Big Fat Rosie handed him the slippers on Christmas morning, he gave her a great big hug. "They're the cuddliest, cosiest slippers I have ever had," he declared, and marched round and round in them, chuckling to himself, like this

LORTLE
ORTLE = ORTLE
ORTLE

Harry came in from the farmyard, waving a sprig of holly. "Merry Christmas!" he said, and presented the holly to Rosie with a deep bow.

Rosie gave him his present, and he thanked her politely. "There's nothing I love, so much as a glove," he told her, wiggling his fingers about with delight.

They all went outside to give the animals their presents. Turnip Tom hung Alexander's bell on the gate of his sty and he pushed at it with his nose. It made a sound like this

and Alexander said, "Oinker oink," which meant "Happy Christmas".

Lollipop put her nose into her green bucket and snorted happily into it, like this

while Annabel nibbled at her carrots and neighed greedily, like this

Maisie, in her yellow ear-warmers, was the most contented cow in the land. She mooed a thank you, like this

and went across the yard to show off her present to the others.

Big Fat Rosie was the only one without a Christmas present. She looked all over the place, but there were no more pretty parcels tied with ribbon. Had they forgotten her?

Turnip Tom and Harry were busy in the farmhouse, decorating the Christmas tree behind a screen. Rosie sat sadly in her rocking chair, thinking: "It's a horrible Christmas, not a bit like my dream. In my dream, I had lots and lots of cream buns for Christmas. Lots and lots and lots . . ."

36

After a while, Turnip Tom came out from behind the screen and sighed, like this

**WHEE-YEW!**

Harry followed him, brushing pine needles from his sleeves and looking as if he were trying to keep a great secret.

"Christmas is supposed to be fun, isn't it," said Big Fat Rosie in a mournful voice. "I mean, everyone gets *presents* at Christmas, don't they. I would have thought *presents* were a very important thing when it's Christmas."

"Shall we show her?" said Turnip Tom to Harry.

"Arr," said Harry.

They pulled aside the screen, and there behind it was an enormous Christmas tree. But this Christmas tree didn't have lights or baubles, or tinsel, or anything like that. From every branch, from every twig, hung a cream bun.

"Happy Christmas, Rosie!" said Turnip Tom.

Big Fat Rosie's eyes grew wider and wider. There were at least fifty buns on the tree. No — sixty! No — a hundred!

"Oh, thank you, thank you, thank you!" she cried. And she began to giggle, like this

**KI-KI-KI-KI-KI**

Then, because she was very, very greedy, Big Fat Rosie wanted to start eating the cream buns there and then.

"Not so fast now, me dear," said Turnip Tom. "Cream buns don't grow on trees, you know."

"Oh yes they do," said Rosie. "On Christmas trees!"

And as they all rolled about with laughter, Big Fat Rosie knew they were going to have the best Christmas ever.

# MUDDLED MESSAGE

*Why not try these two puzzles on your friends?*

Dear Santa
I have got a secret store
of sweets in my toy-box
If you want some creep
into my room after mum
has gone downstairs.
Robert

Can you read this message to Santa? (Hint: you may need to experiment with a mirror!)

# TRICKY TREES

How many Christmas trees can you find in this picture?

# CHRISTMAS DINNER

We were all sitting round the table.
There was roast turkey
there were roast potatoes
there were roast parsnips
there were broccoli tips
there was a dishful of crispy bacon off the turkey
there was wine, cider, beer, lemonade
and milk – for the youngsters.
Everything was set.
It was all on the table.
We were ready to begin.
Suddenly there was a terrible terrible scream.
Right next to the turkey was a worm.
A dirty little worm wriggling about like mad.

For a moment everyone looked at it.
Someone said very quietly, "Oh dear."
And everyone was thinking things like —
"How did it get there?"
"If that came out of the turkey,
I don't want any of it."
or
"I'm not eating any Christmas dinner. It could be full of dirty little wriggly
        worms."

Now — as it happens,
I don't mind wriggly worms.
There was plenty of room for it
at the table.
It was just that . . . that . . .
no one had asked it to come over
for Christmas dinner.

So I said,
"I don't think it came out of the turkey. I think —
It came off the bottom of the milk bottle."
And I picked up the worm,
and put it out the door to spend Christmas day
in a lovely patch of wet mud.
Much nicer place to be —
for a worm.

**Michael Rosen**

# PRESENT PU??LE

Can you help David, Sandra and Leroy find their presents?

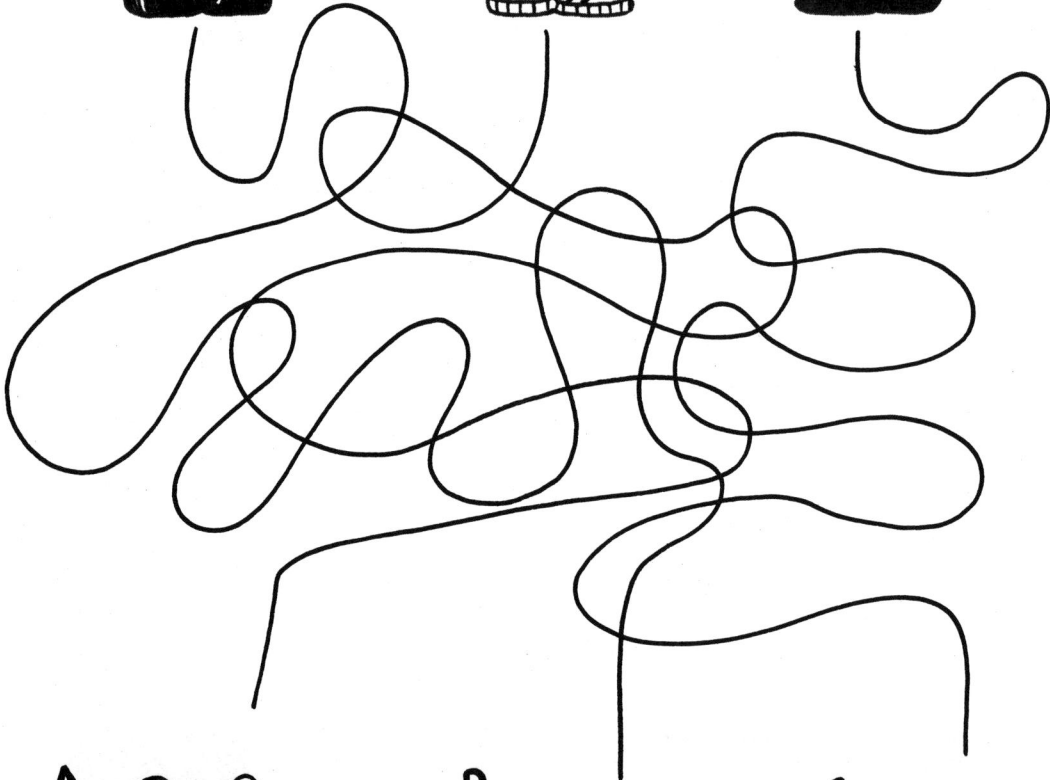

DAVID

SANDRA

LEROY

A

B

C

# PARCEL

When I have a parcel —
Whether it's thick or thin,
When I have a parcel —
Whether it's round or it's square,
Someone says,
"Hey! Stop peeping! Don't you dare!"
So . . .
I just feel it
and feel it
Then shake it a little,
And wonder
and
wonder
What's under the paper.
It's my parcel for Christmas —
I'll open it then,
Just as soon as I can
Get rid of that string!

**Jean Chapman**

What ball doesn't bounce?
*A snowball.*

What exams did Santa take?
*Ho, ho, ho levels.*

What nationality is Santa?
*North Polish.*

# Put Rudolph's Nose in Place

(This is a team game)

**You will need**:
- ★ a scarf for a blindfold
- ★ a large drawing of a reindeer's head or even a whole reindeer (you can draw this in felt-tip)
- ★ a stiff card circle coloured red (this will be the nose)
- ★ some blu-tack to stick the nose in place

**How you play**:
First place the reindeer picture on a wall at about shoulder height. Each person takes a turn to try and put the nose in the right place on the reindeer's face whilst he or she is blindfold. You will need someone to stand by the picture to mark where each person puts the nose. Pencil initials can be used to mark the spot. The winner is the one who puts the nose nearest to the correct position.
*Variations on the game could be*:
Put the hat on the snowman
Put the antlers on the reindeer
Put the robin on the log

# Presents in the Stocking

**You will need**:
- ★ one pair of socks (football socks will be ideal)
- ★ a selection of small items such as: a button; various coins; a small ball etc. (You will need two sets of everything, one for each sock. DON'T USE ANY SHARP THINGS!)

---

What do polar bears eat for a snack?
*Ice-burgers!*

Who claps at Christmas time?
*Santapplause!*

---

**How you play**:
Divide your guests into two teams (if it is a really large party, you can use two pairs of socks and divide into four teams). The game organiser (a grown-up perhaps) calls out an object and the first person in the team runs to the sock, puts in his or her hand and searches for the object purely by feel. If he or she selects the correct one, the item is taken to the organiser who tells that person the name of the next object to look for. (The organiser must keep a check of the objects collected for each team.) The first person then goes back to the team and tells the second player what to feel for.
The winning team is the one which completely empties the stocking first.

# CHRISTMAS PRESENT BOOKMARKS

**You will need:**

★ strips of thin card
★ assorted coloured stickers (red, green and gold if possible)
★ ribbon
★ clear adhesive book covering (optional)

**What you do:**

1 Cut a strip of card. About 16cm by 3cm is a good size.
2 Put your design onto the card. There are all sorts of designs you can create. The illustrations will give you some ideas.
3 To make your bookmark extra special, you can put a personal greeting on the back.
4 Cover the card with clear adhesive book covering if you have some.
5 Make a small hole at the top and tie a piece of ribbon through it.

# CHRISTMAS TREE PAPER CHAINS

**You will need:**

★ one pack of green crepe paper
★ sharp scissors
★ chalk or crayon

**What you do:**

1 When you buy crepe paper, it is usually folded and packed flat.
  When it is still folded, cut the pack in half.
2 Draw your tree design with a chalk or crayon outline. Cut away the
  shaded parts so that it looks like this:
  IMPORTANT: Do *not* cut sharp points or the frieze will fall apart!
3 Open out . . .
  and you've got a wonderful jolly green Christmas tree paper chain!

You can either leave the chain plain or you could decorate the trees with
coloured stickers (like the ones you used to make the bookmarks).
Cut another Christmas tree from the other half of the paper *OR* you could
make a cracker frieze like this:
*You can also make the cracker frieze out of crepe paper in other colours.*

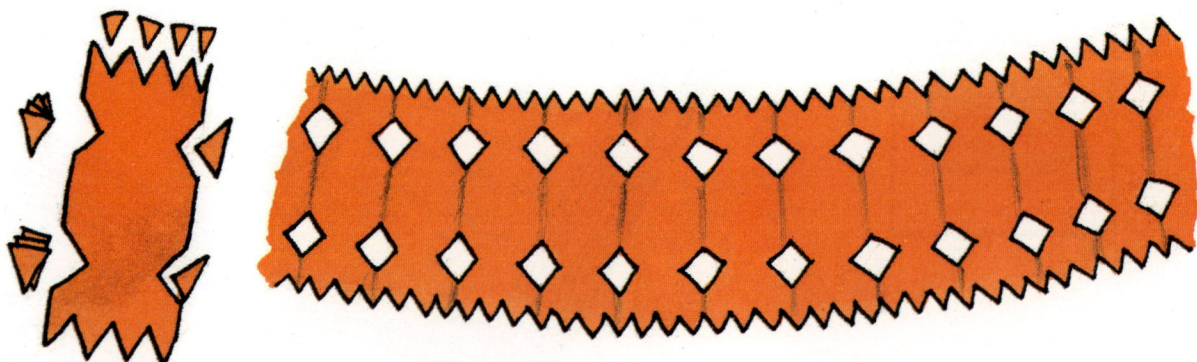

You will have to draw the outlines of the crackers *after* you have cut the shape.

# Ten little Christmas Trees

Ten little Christmas trees a-growing
in a line.
The first went to Bedfordshire,
And that left only nine.

Nine little Christmas trees all found it
long to wait,
The second went to Monmouthshire,
And that left only eight.

Eight little Christmas trees said,
"Christmas will be heaven."
The third went to London Town,
And that left only seven.

Seven little Christmas trees, and all as
straight as sticks!
The fourth went to Oxfordshire,
And that left only six.

Six little Christmas trees, all growing
and alive!
The fifth went to Lancashire,
And that left only five.

Five little Christmas trees said, "Will
they want some more?"
The sixth went to Devonshire,
And that left only four.

Four little Christmas trees, as sturdy as
could be!
The seventh went to Scilly Isles,
And that left only three.

Three little Christmas trees all grew
and grew and grew,
The eighth went to Middlesex,
And that left only two.

Two little Christmas trees, December
almost done!
The ninth went to Timbuctoo,
And that left only one.

One little Christmas tree, feeling very
small!
She came to our school,
and that was best of all.

Ten little Christmas trees, with
Christmas drawing near,
Wish you love and gladness
And a Happy New Year.
**Rodney Bennett**

# DAZZLING DECORATIONS

You can make all sorts of designs and decorations with two simple geometric shapes: circles and squares. How about making some tree decorations like the ones shown here? All you have to do is attach a loop of string at the top and it's ready to hang on your tree!

## WALL HANGING

**You will need:**

★ thin paper or card cut into circles
★ scissors
★ glue
★ pens
★ coloured paper
★ paper plates
★ stickers

**What you do:**

1 On some of your card circles or paper plates, draw pictures and designs with bright colours.
2 On the other circles, you can make patterns with self-adhesive stickers or shapes made out of coloured foil paper which you can glue on.
3 When you have decorated the circles, you can attach them with wide strips of paper which should be about 12cm long. To do this, put a blob of glue on the end of a strip and press this to the back edge of a circle. Do the same with the other end and attach all the plates this way. *You can also make this wall hanging with squares instead. Or how about mixing squares and circles?*

## CHRISTMAS CROWN

How about making a crown to wear to all those Christmas parties?

**You will need:**

★ a strip of card long enough to go around your head
★ small circles of card or paper
★ colouring pencils and felt-tips
★ glue

**What you do:**

1 Create designs on the small circles as you did for the wall hanging.
2 Glue these along the strip of card.
3 Join the card strip at the two ends.
4 Wait for the glue to dry before you put on your crown or it will stick to your head!

# Merry Memory Game

**Look at the picture for one minute**. Now cover it up and try to write down as many things as you can remember seeing in it.

**Another game for your memory**. Look at the picture for one minute, cover it up and try to answer these questions:

1  How many crackers, candles, forks, knives, small cakes, plates in the pile, snowflakes are there?
2  How many different things to eat are there? What are they?
3  What is between the jelly and the candles?
4  What is to the right of the candles?

# It's Christmas

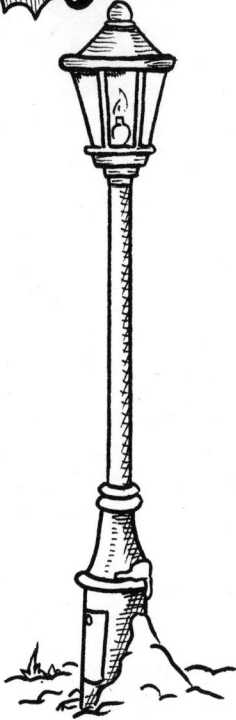

**C**arols drift across the night

**H**olly gleams by candlelight

**R**oaring fire; a spooky tale

**I**ce and snow and wind and hail

**S**anta seen in High Street store

**T**elevision . . . more and more

**M**ince pies, turkey, glass of wine

**A**cting your own pantomime

**S**ocks hung up. It's Christmas time!

**Wes Magee**

# Answers

## Page 12
1 Hark the herald angels sing.
2 Once in royal David's city.
3 Silent night, holy night.
4 While shepherds watched their flocks by night.
5 Rudolph the rednosed reindeer.
6 Away in a manger.
7 Little donkey.
8 Go tell it on the mountain.
9 The cowboy carol.
10 The Virgin Mary had a baby boy.
11 On the first day of Christmas.
12 We wish you a merry Christmas.

## Page 13
Bauble D is the odd one out.

## Page 40
Sandra's present is A, David's is B and Leroy's is C.

## Page 29
**Christmas Code:** BICYCLE, DOLL, TEDDY BEAR, CALCULATOR, BOOKS, CLOTHES

**Christmas Words:** GIFT, TURKEY, CARD

## Page 38
**Muddled Message**

Dear Santa,

I have got a secret store of sweets in my toy box. If you want some creep into my room after Mum has gone down stairs.

Robert

**Tricky Trees:**

There are eleven trees.

# Festivals

# EASTER

## Julian Fox

Wayland

# Festivals

Christmas
Easter
Hallowe'en
Harvest and Thanksgiving

First published in 1984 by
Wayland (Publishers) Limited
49 Lansdowne Place, Hove
East Sussex BN3 1HF, England

ISBN 0 85078 451 4

Phototypeset by The Grange Press, Southwick, Sussex
Printed in Italy by G. Canale & C.S.p.A., Turin
Bound in the U.K. at The Pitman Press, Bath

# Contents

# Celebrating Easter

Everyone knows what happens at Easter. It is a holiday, a time for celebration when schools are closed, shops and factories stop work for a few days, and people enjoy themselves.

Also, in Christian countries, many go to church and remember with sadness the death of Christ, and with joy his coming alive again. It is by far the oldest Christian festival. Some may think Christmas is more important, but there have been times when Christmas was banned by the Church.

For children in many countries, Easter Day means looking for eggs made of chocolate and sugar left by the Easter bunny or hare. In Eastern Europe, people greet each other with three kisses; in Germany, huge bonfires are lit; and in Britain and the U.S.A., hard-boiled hens' eggs are rolled down hills to see which breaks last.

You have probably enjoyed some of these special Easter customs yourself. But have you ever wondered how and why they started? Of course, Christians are happy that Jesus came alive after being killed on the cross, but what has that got to do with new clothes and Easter parades? What have rabbits to do with eggs?

*At Easter, Christians celebrate the coming to life of Jesus three days after his death.*

4

The answer is that Easter is a very, very old festival, originally celebrating the end of winter and the coming of spring. Many of the modern customs we know well were first thought of when people lived in huts and caves. In the following pages, you can find out how it all came about.

*Easter bunnies are a traditional part of Easter.*

5

# The story of Easter

## Spring celebrations

Thousands of years ago, people thought that the sun died in winter and was born again in spring. As the nights lengthened and the weather got colder, children saw their parents look anxiously at the food stores. Nothing grew in the fields, the trees were mostly bare, and no young animals were being born. It was a worrying time.

By mid-winter, the days started to grow longer again. This was a time to celebrate and have parties. Fires were lit and animals were killed and offered as presents to thank the sun gods for bringing a new year. Today, Scots people celebrate Hogmanay at New Year; years ago their Celtic ancestors called it 'Hogenat', which means slaughter night.

*A carving of Adonis, the ancient world's god of spring.*

*There have been many gods of spring. This pagan god was called the Green Man.*

As the winter continued, people did all they could to please the gods. They went without food to show they were not greedy, and they hung branches of evergreen tree over the fields, encouraging the plants to grow again.

Eventually, the days started to last longer than the nights, and it was clear that the sun had really regained its power. The gods of winter and darkness were beaten, and new life was springing up everywhere. This was the time for everyone to have the biggest celebration of the year.

In different parts of the world, people gave different names to the gods they believed had triumphed and brought the world back to life. In the ancient world, now called the Middle East, it was Adonis, who died in winter and was born again in spring. The Romans called their god of spring, Attis. Further north in Europe, people thought the goddess, Eostre, brought the world to life again in spring. Her name later became Easter.

## Pagan rituals

Pagan rituals are the religious ceremonies that took place long ago, before Jesus was born, when people worshipped a variety of other gods and goddesses, including Eostre. The sun was also an important god, and on the day of the spring equinox, when the day became as long as the night, everyone would get up before dawn and go to high ground. As the sun rose they danced and sang, happy that the winter was over.

In ancient Egypt and countries nearby, the death and rebirth of Adonis, god of spring, was celebrated in the feast of Adonia, which lasted eight days. And every March the Romans held a sad procession to mourn the death of their god, Attis, followed by carnivals and feasting after the equinox, when he was supposed to have come alive again.

*Today, morris dancers perform ritual dances which are relics of pagan forms of worship.*

Imagine you are living in a pagan tribe long ago. It is March, it is the day of the spring festival, and you have just walked down from the hilltop where the dawn bonfire still smoulders. Soon you will dress up for a parade through the village to the magic tree. It is a silent march on an empty stomach – no-one has eaten yet – but all the children carry painted eggs, to give to each other, as symbols of new life.

The old oak tree is hung with evergreen branches of mistletoe and with spring flowers; around the tree are a bull and some lambs. When everyone is in place, the chiefs and holy men kill the animals and chant to the sky, praying for good crops and lots of children to be born. Then everyone sings and is happy. Food and drink are brought out and all the tribe celebrates the death of winter, and the birth of spring.

*At the spring festival, the Celts celebrated the death of winter and the birth of spring.*

## Christianity's main festival

When Christianity first spread across Europe, believers in the new faith changed many of the older rites and ceremonies, adapting them to fit in with the life and teaching of Jesus. They did not try to stop people having a great spring event for their old pagan goddess, Eostre; what they did

*A Holy Week procession in Brazil.*

*In Sweden, girls wear crowns of candles during the festival of spring.*

was quickly turn the festival into the most important event in the new religion.

Easter ceased to be the festival of nature being renewed by spring, and became the time for people to renew their faith in Jesus and God.

Instead of sacrificing animals, praying to the goddess of spring, and giving each other eggs to represent new life, people were taught to remember God's sacrifice of Jesus on the cross, and then celebrate his coming back to life three days later.

Eggs were said to represent the stone that was mysteriously moved from the cave holding Christ's body. Fires were lit in churches and candles were burnt to symbolize the light spread by the word of God, not the power of the sun.

In those early years, Easter was held at different times by different groups of Christians, but in AD 325 an important council decided that Easter Day should be the first Sunday after the first full moon, following the spring equinox. This was later agreed by everyone and the rule is still used today.

As the years went by, Christians fitted Easter into a longer and more complicated pattern of events. First came the self-denial and hard times of Lent, leading into the contrasting sadness and joy of Easter week, and finally the period leading up to Ascension Day and Whitsun.

Today, for most people Easter starts with Palm Sunday, and ends eight days later with the Easter Monday public holiday. Christians call this period Holy Week.

# Holy Week

## Palm Sunday

Holy Week for Christians starts with a traditional day of rejoicing – Palm Sunday. It commemorates the day when Jesus Christ rode into Jerusalem on a donkey and was greeted by large crowds of his supporters and believers, who shouted praise and called him King. They tore branches down from roadside palm trees, waved them in their excitement and threw them on the ground to make a path for him to ride over.

Blessing and giving out palm-leaf crosses is still the custom in Roman Catholic churches, but most Protestant churches have given up this custom. In

*On Palm Sunday, Christians remember the entry of Jesus into Jerusalem.*

Britain and northern countries where palm trees will not grow, evergreen branches of yew, hazel or willow are often used to decorate the church.

Until recently, children used to go into the countryside for several days before Palm Sunday to gather green branches. They decorated their own houses and cottages, as well as the church, and also wore little sprigs of green in their button-holes.

In Spain it is warm enough for palm trees to grow, and millions of crosses for Palm Sunday are made in the town of Elche. While they are still growing on the tree, the thin fronds at the top of male palms are specially cut and folded so that they shade other fibres chosen to make the crosses. These strands become quite white.

In other countries, there are lots more Palm Sunday customs. In Italy, olive branches are used instead of palms; in Jerusalem, processions follow the route Jesus took originally; and in parts of West Germany, the priest used to ride to church on a donkey.

*Children holding palm fronds during a Palm Sunday procession in Spain.*

# Maundy Thursday

The Bible tells us that on the day before he was killed, Jesus washed the feet of his disciples to show that even the most important people should be humble, and he gave them a new commandment. The old Latin word for command was *mandatum*, and this was shortened over the years into 'maundy'.

*Jesus washing the feet of Peter, one of his disciples.*

In later years, priests used to wash the feet of twelve poor people to show they had learnt this lesson of humility, and afterwards gave out small gifts of money or food. As time went by, the ceremony became grander and even kings took it up.

Austrian emperors, helped by archdukes, used to wash the feet of twelve old men, and then serve food to them at a magnificent dinner on Maundy Thursday. A similar event took place in Russia before the Revolution, and in France and Spain.

Clothes as well as money were given to poor people by the king in England. The number of those receiving gifts depended on the age of the giver. So on his fiftieth birthday, Edward III washed a hundred feet.

In England today, one old man and one old woman for each year of the Queen's age take part in a fine ceremony when the Queen gives them coloured leather purses containing specially-minted coins (feet are not washed these days). The 'Maundy money' coins can be spent in shops, but they are usually kept as special souvenirs of the occasion.

The Maundy celebration is also held by the Pope in Rome. He washes the feet of thirteen priests, and then serves them bread and wine. The number is made up of the twelve disciples together with one who represents an angel.

Maundy Thursday clearly originated with Christianity, and has no link with earlier beliefs or religions.

*On Maundy Thursday in Britain, the Queen gives a group of pensioners some specially-minted coins.*

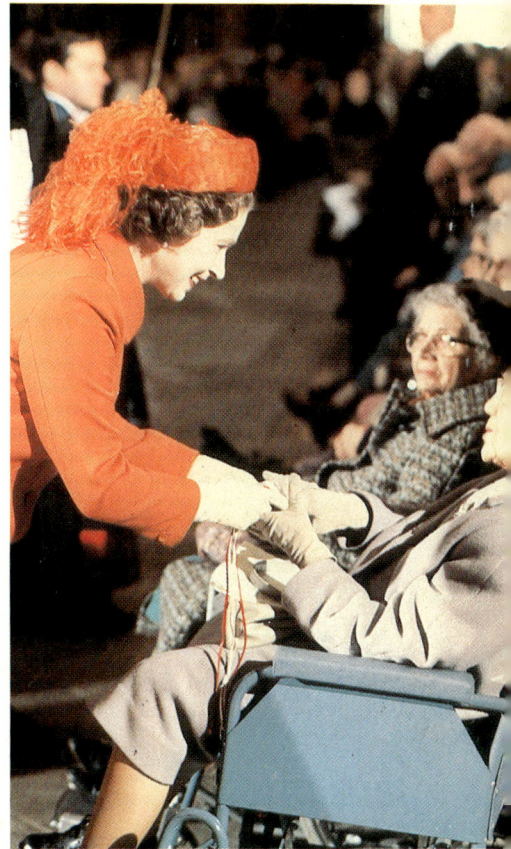

# Good Friday

This day is at the heart of the Easter event – the day on which Jesus Christ was killed. For Christians, it is a day of fasting and sorrow, when God's sacrifice of his Son is remembered. Many feel sorry for wrong things they have done in the past,

*A Good Friday procession with a tableau of Jesus carrying the cross on which he died.*

*In Mexico, Christians often wear black on Good Friday.*

and ask God to forgive them, remembering that Jesus said he would carry the burden of their sins.

You may wonder why a day of sadness in memory of an innocent man being executed is called 'Good' Friday. Some say that it came from an older label, 'God's' Friday; others say it started in days when 'Good' meant 'Holy'. Danes called it 'Long' Friday in their language, and in some European countries it is 'Great' Friday.

Whatever its name, Good Friday is thought an unlucky day in all Christian countries. Until recently, miners refused to go below ground and fishermen would not set sail on that day. Men, such as blacksmiths, who used iron in their work, stayed at home because iron nails had been used to pin Jesus to the cross.

It is said that there are still some women in Europe who will do no washing on Good Friday. According to the old superstition, blood stains would appear on any clothes and linen laundered on that day.

On the other hand, many believed it was a good day to plant seeds, saying that this was one time Satan had no power to stop plants growing well. Does this remind you of those older pre-Christian customs?

Nowadays, most of these superstitions are forgotten, but Good Friday is still a sad day for millions. Millions more eat hot cross buns for breakfast on Good Friday, as we will see later.

## Easter Day

Lighting fires, pealing bells, eating chocolate eggs, singing hymns, giving presents, feasting and rejoicing: they are all part of Easter Day celebrations. Following the gloom of Good Friday, this is the joyful part of the great Easter festival.

Churches that have been kept bare and bleak are decorated with flowers and greenery – white lillies, white narcissi and evergreen yew are thought specially appropriate as Christians celebrate their holiest of days. For them, it is the greatest day of the year, more important even than Christmas. They remember the day when Mary Magdalene went to the tomb where Jesus was buried, and found the stone at its mouth rolled away. The body was gone, and Mary learned from two angels that Jesus had risen and was alive again.

For believers this was a wonderful event, which proved that Jesus really was the true son of God. And it is not surprising that Christians started celebrating the resurrection instead of the older gods and goddesses of spring.

There is no doubt that Jesus's ordeal happened at the same time of year when the Jews had their Passover celebration. Passover was always celebrated near the time of the spring equinox, although the day in the week varied. It is connected to Easter in several ways. You may have heard the word 'Paschal' used about things to do with

*This old print shows Russian villagers giving their friends and neighbours Easter eggs on Easter Day.*

18

Easter. It comes from the Hebrew word for Passover, *Pesakh*.

From that word also comes the French for Easter, *Pâcques*, together with Spanish, Dutch, Italian and Swedish words for it. In the north of England, Easter eggs are often called Pace Eggs – another variation – and Pace Egg Plays are performed. If you are Scottish you may talk of Paiss or Peace Eggs.

*Easter Day is the holiest of days for Christians.*

## Easter Monday

After the two great days of religious celebration – Good Friday and Easter Sunday – comes the day that has for centuries been the occasion for sports and traditional outdoor games, Easter Monday. Nowadays, it is widely held as a public holiday, and there are all sorts of professional sports entertainments, such as football matches and motor races.

One of the oldest customs for children is egg rolling – hard-boiled eggs or imitation wooden eggs being rolled down hillsides to see which reaches the bottom first, or rolls the farthest. Games for older boys and girls included splashing each other with water, wrestling for pieces of meat pie, and playing various ball games. In one English town, there were so many games played that the day after Easter was called Ball Monday.

*An old Dutch picture of villagers performing an 'egg dance'.*

Our Easter holiday usually ends after the Monday, but years ago nobody worked on the second Monday and Tuesday after Easter, either. This was called Hocktide, and saw two more days of sports and celebrations, some of them very rough. For instance, on the Monday, gangs of women would take ropes and capture any man they came across, insisting on a small amount of money from the victim before he was released. Next day it was the men's turn, and they would sometimes stretch a rope across the road and stop anyone passing, tying them up until the money was handed over. The proceeds were supposed to go towards maintaining the church, but were occasionally given to poor people as well.

It is many years since these 'binding' games were played. What do you think would happen if a vicar or priest tried to raise money by starting them up again?

*Motor racing is just one of many sports held on Easter Monday.*

# Hares, rabbits and eggs

Osterbruss aus Leipzig

Leipzig 2km.

Eierhandlung von O. HASE.

## Hares and rabbits

All over Europe, there are children who get up early on Easter Day and search through gardens and odd corners of their homes looking for Easter

*This German Easter card of 1906 shows rabbits or hares loading up large baskets with freshly-painted eggs.*

Eggs. Maybe you do? Maybe you were told when you were very young, that the eggs were hidden overnight by the Easter hare or rabbit? You may be older now and no longer believe in Santa Claus or the Easter hare, but have you ever wondered how the story started? After all, birds lay eggs, animals do not!

The answer is that the Easter hare was no ordinary animal, but a sacred companion of the old goddess of spring, Eostre. Since long before Jesus Christ was born, parents told their children that the magic hare would run through the night and bring them presents at the spring festival. The presents were often painted hens' eggs, as these represented the new life starting at this time of year.

Hares have always been solitary and rather mysterious animals, quite unlike rabbits in behaviour. In some countries they were rare and people confused them with rabbits, which were smaller but similar to look at. That is why some people now think of the Easter bunny. In North America, for instance, the Easter rabbit has completely taken over from the original hare.

The presents brought and hidden by the animal are usually chocolate eggs, and in some countries, such as Yugoslavia, children go outdoors before Easter and prepare little nests ready for the hare. In West Germany and Hungary, children have small baskets decorated with hares, specially to collect eggs and small gifts at Easter.

From the same tradition, pictures of hares and rabbits are often used to decorate Easter cards and the wrapping paper used for chocolate and cardboard eggs.

*A small child with an Easter basket.*

## Easter eggs

It is easy to understand why so many people see the egg as a symbol of spring – the new life is right there inside the shell. Can you think of anything else that might stand so well for birth and the start of growing?

The old primitive people living thousands of years ago certainly could not. In China, India, Persia, Greece and Egypt, the old civilizations ate eggs during the spring festivals, and used their shape in pictures and decorations to show fertility.

The early Christians agreed with this. They brought eggs to church for blessing by the priest as holy symbols of Christ's rebirth. An old story suggests that Jesus's mother painted eggs for her baby to play with, and although probably not true, it is still told to children in Poland, rather like a fairy story.

Painting hens' eggs is a very old practice. There are records of Chinese people giving each other red eggs at the spring festival almost 3,000 years ago. Sometimes very detailed designs were drawn on the shells to make the eggs more precious, and this practice continued right up until about a hundred years ago.

That was when the first artificial eggs of sugar and marzipan were made. Then came the chocolate Easter egg, which became so popular that today you might live through several Easters and

*Cardboard eggs containing small presents were very popular a hundred years ago.*

24

never see another kind. The next most popular is probably the decorated cardboard shell in two parts, which can hold a small present.

Remember next Easter that whatever sort of eggs you have, they are still symbols of spring and new life just as they always have been.

*You can still buy decorated cardboard eggs.*

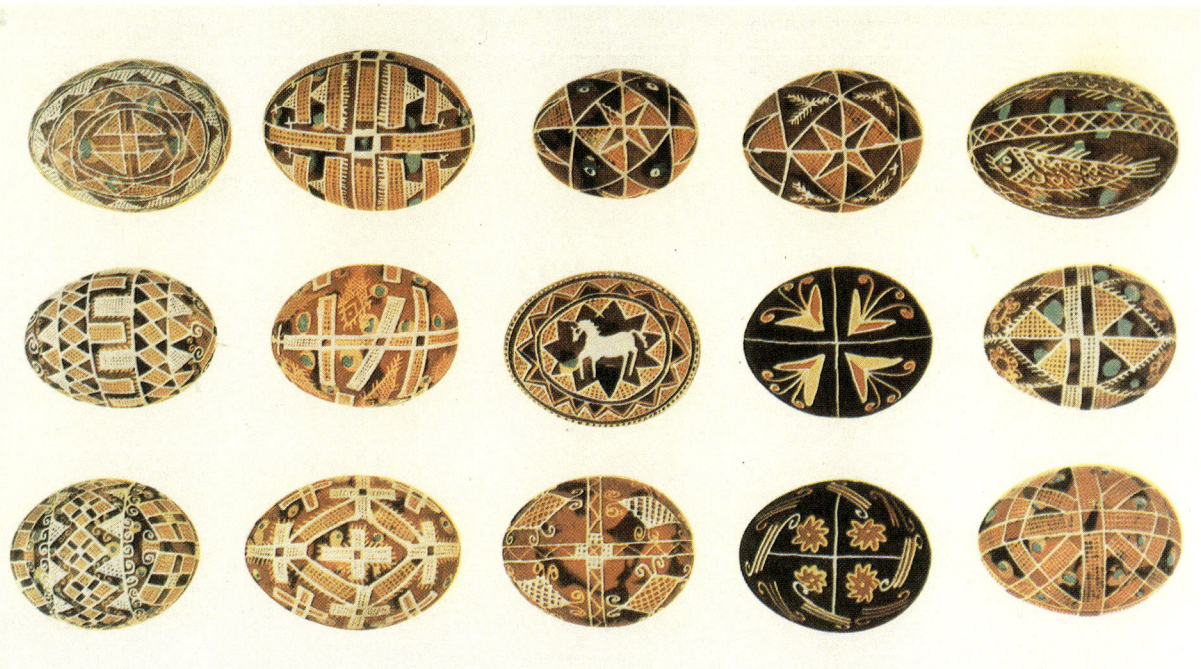

## Decorating eggs

Red is probably the favourite colouring for Easter eggs – some say it represents the blood of Christ – but any colour will do. The simplest method is to put a little edible dye into the water the eggs are boiled in. Most food shops sell suitable vegetable dyes in little bottles.

You can also use natural dyes. Spinach in the water turns eggs green, beetroot turns them red, tea dyes them dark brown, and onion skin a golden colour. It is best to use an old saucepan for colouring eggs, as your mother might be angry if you turned the inside of her best new pan red or green!

The Swiss and Scandinavians achieve a very pleasing effect by wrapping onion skin round the eggs before boiling, sometimes with small leaves and flowers underneath. This makes a very pretty white pattern on the golden brown shell.

*These highly-decorated hens' eggs from West Germany were painted in 1909.*

An easy way to get the same sort of effect is to draw a pattern on a boiled egg with a white wax crayon – taking care not to break the shell – and then dipping the egg in dye. The wax keeps the dye away and the pattern stays the same colour as the original shell.

Of course, you can always hard-boil the egg in plain water and then paint on it afterwards when it cools. That is probably the easiest way of achieving the design you want.

There is nothing to stop you painting a face on the hard-boiled egg and then gluing cotton wool on for a beard, or giving the head some hair with short pieces of wool. With two small pieces of felt for ears, and some cotton for whiskers, you could even make an Easter hare.

*Painting hens' eggs at Easter is easy and fun to do.*

# Egg games

Rolling Easter eggs down a slope is a game children have played for thousands of years. The tradition still goes on, particularly in northern England, Scotland, Switzerland and America. Back in 1877, the American President's wife, Mrs. Madison, taught American children how to roll eggs. Ever since huge crowds of children are allowed into the gardens of the White House in Washington on Easter Monday, when more than 100,000 eggs are rolled. The most famous area in England for egg rolling is Lancashire.

Another egg game, familiar to many boys in northern England and elsewhere, is 'egg-shackling'. This is played like conkers: each of the two players holds a hard-boiled egg in his hand, then they bang them together until one breaks. It is a

*Egg games have been a part of the spring celebrations for thousands of years.*

very old game and used to be widespread, but now it is just played in a few parts of Europe.

On Easter Sunday in Greece, a brightly-coloured egg is carried around in the hand, and when two people meet they knock their eggs together (not hard enough to break them) and say, 'Christ is risen'. The traditional game for French children is to throw an egg in the air and catch it. The first player to drop an egg on the ground is the loser.

You might wonder why anyone should play with eggs at all – it certainly does not make them better to eat! According to historians, the answer goes right back to primitive times. Egg rolling and shackling are simple games left over from spring festivals, which probably involved much more complicated egg rituals. These were performed to ensure the fields grew good crops, and also that the young women would bear lots of children.

*An egg-rolling competition on the lawns of the White House is about to start.*

# Customs and games

## Lifting and ducking

Whether in pagan or Christian times, Easter has always been an occasion for taking part in sports and games. Nowadays, it might be football, rugby or horse-racing, but the old traditions included some very strange customs, which once again can be traced back to the days of primitive man.

Take lifting, for instance – a very popular sport all over Europe until well into the last century, and one which started as a magic rite to make crops grow tall.

On Easter Monday, groups of young men decorated chairs with evergreen branches and

*Lifting was popular all over Europe until about 150 years ago.*

*Horse-racing is a popular Easter sport.*

ribbons, then carried them round the neighbourhood. Women and girls had to sit in the chairs, and be lifted high in the air three times before paying a little money or gift to be released. On the next day, it was the women's turn to lift the men.

This was originally a gentle and good-humoured game. But in the towns, things got rougher – the young men did not bother with chairs, and simply threw strangers and friends into the air and refused to let them go until they had paid. Magistrates tried to ban lifting but failed, and it was only with changing times that it died out.

Water was a part of some games, and in Eastern Europe, Easter Monday was often called Ducking Monday. It was the day on which unmarried girls were grabbed and thrown into ponds or lakes – where there were no ponds or lakes, buckets of water were tipped over them. The girls were expected to take this in fun, and were told it would make them better wives and more likely to have children.

31

## Hallaton's Easter games

If you think lifting people into the air or throwing them into water are strange kinds of sport, what about hare-pie scrambling and bottle-kicking? These are the Easter games at Hallaton in Leicestershire, and despite the name, there is no hare in the pie and no bottles are kicked.

Instead, the rector cuts up a large beef pie and the slices are carried in procession to a piece of ground called Hare Pie Bank. There the pieces are thrown into a crowd of people, who scrum around trying to grab a bit.

The 'bottles' are really small, wooden barrels of beer, which have been solemnly carried to Hare Pie Bank in the procession along with the sack of

*Bottle-kicking is an odd game played every Easter Monday at Hallaton.*

32

pie pieces. The bottle-kicking starts after the pie has been scrambled. Men from Hallaton compete against a team from other villages in trying to kick the beer barrels in opposite directions over the boundary lines nearly a mile apart. It is a rough game that lasts a long time, and any number of players can take part.

When it is over, the winner's captain is hoisted into the air and given first drink of the beer before the other barrels are emptied and noisily drunk. Then if they are not too badly damaged, the barrels are put away and kept until the next Easter Monday. No-one knows how these games started, and various kill-joys who have tried to stop them have had no success.

Easier to understand, perhaps, is the playing of all sorts of ball games, which has always been common all over Europe. Skittles, football, stoolball and handball are just some of the games played, and maybe there is a connection with the Easter egg games and the early spring rites.

*Ball games, including football, are played at Easter.*

## Foods and feasting

Food plays an important part in the Easter celebrations, starting with the hot cross buns eaten on Good Friday. If you have read through this book, by now you will not be surprised to learn that buns like these were familiar at Easter-time spring festivals long before Jesus was crucified.

Crosses were used as signs by pagans, and were baked on cakes used in worship of the goddess Diana, for instance. Now they remind Christians of Christ's suffering. An old superstition held that hot cross buns had to be baked on Good Friday itself, and both bakers and housewives would get up specially early to have them ready for breakfast. Today, they are usually made days before, and just heated up again on Good Friday. Unlike some of the old Easter customs, which are dying out, eating hot cross buns is as popular as ever in Europe, and they are also eaten throughout North America.

For lunch on Easter Day, roast lamb is most frequently eaten – a habit dating back to the Jewish Passover. In Italy the lamb often goes with a special salad made with hard-boiled eggs, and in other countries, veal and special large custard tarts are traditional.

Easter Day food is treated most seriously in eastern Europe. Polish Catholic families, in particular, cover the kitchen table with evergreen leaves, and then pile it high with all the best meats, vegetables and sweets they can find. Of course, they include hard-boiled eggs, often

*A ring of Paschal bread from Crete.*

34

decorated by clever artists who are paid for their skilful and complicated designs. Before anything on the table can be eaten it must first be blessed by the local priest. In towns, priests cannot get round to everyone, so children of Catholic families get the job of carrying samples of the food to church to be blessed.

*It is traditional for hot cross buns to be baked early on Good Friday.*

## Parades and processions

In spring, as the weather becomes warmer and the days grow longer, people seem to enjoy putting on new clothes, taking a special interest in how they look. Easter has always been an occasion for people to dress up and take part in parades and processions.

Until recently, everyone wore hats, and it was easy for rich and poor alike at Easter to cover their hats and bonnets with flowers and bows. Such bonnets were often very elaborate, and the best won prizes in Easter bonnet competitions.

There are still some famous Easter parades where prizes are awarded to the best-dressed people. One is in Atlantic City on the east coast of America, another is in Battersea Park, London.

The biggest show of dressing up and the longest processions are held in Spain, particularly in the

*A colourful Easter parade in New York, U.S.A.*

*An Easter procession of cloaked men walk through the Spanish city of Madrid.*

southern city of Seville. From Palm Sunday to Good Friday, huge floats, representing scenes from the Bible story of Easter, are carried slowly through the streets. Some weigh nearly half a tonne and need forty men to carry them! Walking alongside are men, many of them barefoot, wearing strange black or white hoods and cloaks, to show they are sorry for past sins.

Afterwards, there is one of the world's largest spring fairs in Seville. For days, everyone dances and sings until late at night. Work stops, musicians play in the street, and everyone is dressed in their best clothes for the *feria*.

Years ago, the Spaniards conquered parts of South America, and cities in Mexico and elsewhere still celebrate Easter with exciting and colourful *ferias*.

# Fires and fireworks

When you remember that Easter was once the time to rejoice because the cold days of winter were over, you can easily understand why our ancestors lit huge bonfires to show the sun and other gods that they were grateful to be warm again.

In northern countries, such as Sweden and West Germany, they still do, and for many children there the best part of Easter is going out in the evening to play round the bonfire and watch fireworks. Some believe that the fireworks will scare away witches and evil spirits.

Another day on which bonfires are lit, is Good Friday. In many parts of Europe, particularly Portugal, dolls representing Judas, the betrayer of Jesus, are burned in the flames. Some burn a straw doll in the fire, representing winter being burnt up by the new spring.

Christians have used fire in several different ways at Easter as a symbol of the new light and understanding spread by Jesus. There are places in the countryside where all fires were put out on Easter Saturday, and only relit the next day with burning sticks taken from a special fire blessed by the priest. Nowadays, a similar fire is sometimes used to light candles for the church.

Many churches, Roman Catholic and Greek Orthodox in particular, hold a special service on the Saturday night before Easter Day. As the worshippers gather inside, the whole building is

*On Good Friday many years ago, Portuguese sailors used to flog effigies of Judas with sticks.*

*A candlelit Easter service in the Epiphany Cathedral in Moscow, Russia.*

kept in darkness until everyone is ready. Then the priest strikes one small light, and everyone remembers how Jesus came out of his dark tomb.

After the one light has been blessed, it is used first to light a very large candle and then other smaller ones until the whole church is bright again. The large single candle, called the Paschal Candle, stays lit for the next forty days until Ascension Day, when Jesus is said to have gone up to Heaven.

# Passion plays

*A Polish Good Friday Passion play.*

Long before books were printed and most people learned to read, history was learned by listening to stories. The most important story for Christians was Christ's Passion – the Holy Week ending in his resurrection. To help everyone remember this story in detail, the main events were acted out in Passion plays, usually on Good Friday.

These took place in village churches and halls all over Europe, but in one village in West Germany they became specially famous. It happened like this.

Hundreds of years ago a plague, called the Black Death, was killing thousands of people, and in 1633 the villagers of Oberammergau became stricken by it. As an expression of their gratitude for the end of the plague, the villagers vowed to God that they would act a Passion play every ten years. And to this day they have kept their promise.

Today, so many people want to watch the play that it has to take place in an enormous open-air theatre, able to seat 5,000 people at a time. But it is still acted by the villagers. Every tenth year, a cast of about 400 give two performances a week, backed by a large symphony orchestra. The play is very long – nearly five hours – so it is performed in two parts, with lunch in between.

Rehearsals start about two years in advance and, for months before the opening night, the men grow long hair and beards like the people in the Passion story. The only actor to cut his hair is the man chosen to play Pontius Pilate – he was a Roman who would have had short hair and no beard.

Although the Oberammergau Passion play is very much an Easter story, it is nowadays played in summer when the weather is likely to be fine for the huge outdoor audiences.

*A young girl dressed as an angel for a Passion play.*

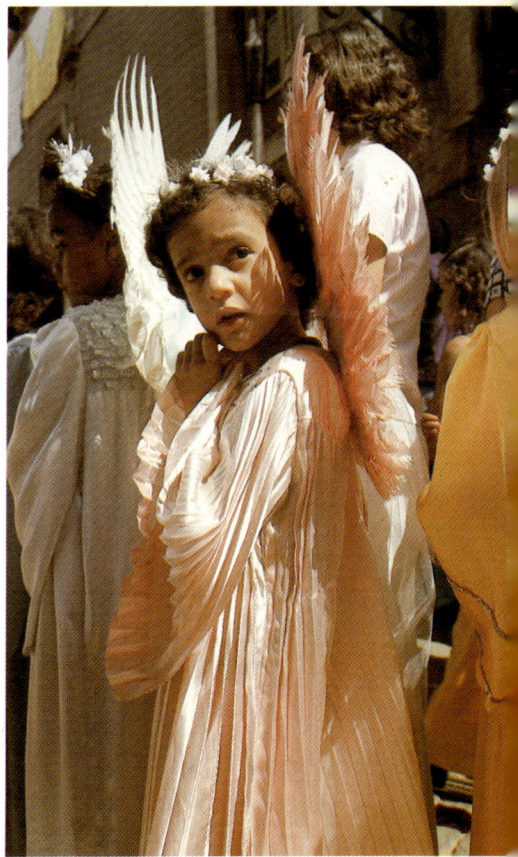

# Spring festivals around the world

*Spring festivals in Japan are always very colourful.*

We have seen in this book how the old spring festivals of Europe and the Middle East were taken over by the Christian Church; how newer beliefs were added and old customs adapted, forming the Easter holiday we know today. But what happens in countries with different religious beliefs – do they have spring festivals?

*Hindus covered in coloured powder during their festival of* Holi.

The answer is, yes. They have different names, of course, but spring festivals are held in just about every country in the world.

In China, for instance, the spring festival is called *Ch'ing Ming*, meaning 'Pure Brightness'. It is among the oldest of the Chinese festivals, and is one that has survived despite big changes in government and the way of life for Chinese people at home and abroad.

Japan celebrates *Setsubun*, 'Change of Season', at this time of year, with ceremonies in its homes and in temples. Roast beans are scattered around homes and in the streets in the old belief that devils and evil spirits will be driven away, allowing the new season to start well.

The spring harvest comes earlier in India, so the festival of *Holi* is held by Hindus in late February or early March, but it is clearly a spring occasion. Fires play a very important part; bright clothes are worn; people spray coloured water or powder on each other; and there are processions and dancing in the streets. For Sikhs in India, the festival is called *Hola-Mohalla*, and the emphasis is on sports and physical games in a kind of fair which last three days.

Remember that for some Christians, Easter does not happen in the spring at all. For Australians in the southern hemisphere, Easter falls at the end of their summer, so Easter shows are more like European harvest festivals with sports and games added on. But they still hide Easter eggs for children to find.

# Easter in the future

For thousands of years, the Easter spring festival has been held to celebrate the end of winter, and to pray for new crops of food and more livestock. We can see that Easter has always been of great importance to rural people, farmers and farm-workers. Even in the small towns and cities of the past, the value of good crops and livestock was well understood.

But with the recent growth of large towns and cities, many of the old Easter customs have faded away. Even in the countryside, machines and science have largely replaced workers, and people no longer pray for enough to eat.

So now that starvation and winter cold are not a common threat to life – in Europe and North America at least – will Easter itself fade away? It is possible, of course, but there are at least two reasons why it is likely to keep going.

One is religious: Easter Week is the most dramatic week in the Christian year and will undoubtedly be celebrated wherever the Christian faith can be found. The other is people's need to forget work and enjoy themselves.

*Easter will always be celebrated by Christians the world over.*

So if, in the future, you spend Easter with your children or grand-children, you can remember this book and tell them why they are hunting for eggs on the first Sunday after the first full moon following the spring equinox.

*Easter parades are enjoyed by people of all ages.*

# Glossary

**Ascension Day** The day on which Christians celebrate the passing of Jesus Christ from earth into heaven.

**Celts** A group of people who inhabited most of Europe in pre-Roman times.

**Commandment** An order or law given by God; one of the Ten Commandments of the Old Testament.

**Equinox** The time in each year when day and night have equal length.

**Evergreen** A tree or shrub that stays green throughout the year.

**Lent** A time when Christians fast in commemoration of Jesus's fast in the wilderness.

**Pagan** A heathen; a person who is not a Christian, Jew or Muslim.

**Passion play** A play which acts out the Easter story of Jesus.

**Passover** An annual feast of the Jews in memory of the Israelites escape from Egypt.

**Rite** A solemn event, such as a religious service.

**Ritual** A set way of performing a religious service.

**Superstition** A misguided belief in magic and irrational fears.

**Symbol** Something that represents or stands for something.

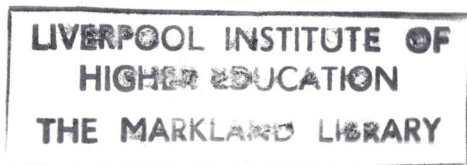

# Further reading

If you would like to find out more about Easter, you may like to read the following books:

*Festivals and Saints Days* by Victor J. Green (Blandford Press, 1978)

*Easter and its Customs* by Christina Hole (Richard Bell)

*The Easter Book* by Jenny Vaughan (Macdonald Educational, 1980)

*The Easter Story in Stained Glass* illustrated by Sonia Halliday and Laura Lushington (Lion, 1980)

*A Book of Spring* by Colin and Moira Maclean (Cassell Collier Macmillan, 1975)

*Fairs and Revels* by Brian Jewell (Midas Books, 1976)

# Index

# Acknowledgements

The publisher would like to thank all those who provided pictures on the following pages:
Bruce Coleman Limited 4, 10, 13, 17, 21, 36, 37, 41, 42, 44; Mary Evans Picture Library 12,
14, 18, 22, 24, 26, 30, 38; Outlook Films Ltd. 11; Ann & Bury Peerless 43; PHOTRI 5, 23, 29;
Picturepoint Ltd. 16, 19, 34, 40, 45; Ronald Sheridan's Photo-Library 6, 7; Syndication
International 15; TASS 39; TOPHAM cover, 25; Malcolm S. Walker 27, 32, 35; ZEFA 31, 33.